No AR

T5-AQQ-562

Everything You Need To Know About

EATING DISORDERS

ANOREXIA AND BULIMIA

An eating disorder can make any meal an uncomfortable experience.

• THE NEED TO KNOW LIBRARY •

Everything You Need To Know About

EATING DISORDERS

ANOREXIA AND BULIMIA

Rachel Kubersky, M.P.H.

THE ROSEN PUBLISHING GROUP, INC.
NEW YORK

Published in 1992, 1996, 1998 by The Rosen Publishing Group, Inc.
29 East 21st Street, New York, NY 10010

Revised Edition 1998
Copyright © 1992, 1996, 1998 by The Rosen Publishing Group, Inc.

Library of Congress Cataloging-in-Publication Data

Kubersky, Rachel.
    Everything you need to know about eating disorders / Rachel Kubersky
(The Need to know library)
    Includes bibliographical references and index.
    Summary: Discusses eating disorders, the role of food in our lives, and how to stay healthy physically and mentally.
    ISBN 0-8239-2838-1
    1. Anorexia nervosa—Juvenile literature. [1. Bulimia—Juvenile literature.
[1. Anorexia nervosa 2. Bulimia. 3. Eating disorders. 4. Food—Psychological aspects.] I. Title. II. Series.
RC552.A5K83   1998
616.85'26—dc20
                                                          91-46600
                                                            CIP
                                                            AC

Manufactured in the United States of America

Contents

Introduction

*I*t was Friday night, and Deidre was hanging out with her friends Janeen, Tisha, and Emily. They had ordered a pizza and were settling down to watch a movie. Deidre was reaching for a slice when the movie began. The opening scene showed a skinny blonde in a bikini. One by one, the girls dropped their slices of pizza.

"Oh, great! I feel like such a pig now," Emily said.

"Yeah, no kidding," said Tisha. "I'd probably have to work out every day for six months without eating a thing to become that skinny."

"My sister told me that some of her friends use laxatives to help them lose weight," Janeen said.

"Really?" Deidre asked. "Do they work? I've tried everything to get rid of my huge stomach, and nothing has helped."

"Oh, shut up! You are so thin," said Janeen. "I'm the one who has to lose some weight."

Soon Deidre's friends started talking about other things, but Deidre was already making plans to go to the drugstore to buy some laxatives after school the next day. She was willing to try anything to lose weight.

Deidre may be on her way to developing an eating disorder. Young people are especially at risk for eating disorders. During adolescence, teens face physical and emotional changes, pressures from friends, and messages about beauty from television, movies, and advertisements. Teens are constantly being sent messages by the media saying that being thin is the ideal. Because of this, some begin to associate physical appearance—and thinness—with happiness.

In this book you will learn about the two most common eating disorders: anorexia nervosa and bulimia nervosa. It will explain what these disorders are, why a person develops them, their consequences, and ways to recover from these dangerous eating disorders. This book will also discuss the role that food plays in people's lives and why so many teenagers are obsessed with losing weight.

If you think that you may have an eating disorder, it is critically important to recognize your problem and find help. Left untreated, an eating disorder can cause serious illness and even death. For example, Karen Carpenter, a well-known pop singer, died from heart failure, a common result of anorexia nervosa.

Eating disorders can be devastating, but you can recover. Better yet, you can prevent yourself from developing one. This book will help you to understand eating disorders and make healthy choices about your body.

For many teens, rituals surrounding food are an important part of being social.

Chapter 1

Food: Many Meanings

A man cannot be too serious about his eating, for food is the force that binds society together.

–Confucius

Food is a necessary part of human life. Human beings need food to survive. Food gives fuel to the body to carry on its normal functions. If your body does not have enough food, it will not work well physically or mentally. If you do not eat for a long period of time, you will die.

Besides its importance for nutrition, food plays other roles in people's lives. To some, food is a source of comfort and pleasure. Memories of grandma's homemade apple pie may bring back happy feelings. For many people, food can also relieve stress and anxiety. Snacking on a sugary cupcake may make you feel better after a bad day. Different foods can symbolize many different things.

Food and Feelings

Food may also influence your emotions. Most of us associate certain foods with certain feelings. For example, some foods may give you the feeling of being cared for. For some people that food might be chicken soup. For others it might be mashed potatoes or macaroni and cheese. Someone else may associate this feeling of safety and well-being with chocolate ice cream or cooked greens.

Foods that make you feel cared for are often called "comfort foods." Your feelings about foods usually develop at an early age.

It is easy to understand why we often associate food with comfort. Your earliest experience with food involved being held, cared for, and fed. Whether you were fed from a bottle or from your mother's breast, you were held close. The good feeling of being held was linked to being fed.

Your need to be fed also made your parents listen to you. When you cried, you told those taking care of you that you were hungry. Then you were not only fed, but also held close.

Food and Traditions

Food and drink, from the earliest times, have played an important part in all sorts of celebrations. Certain sweet spices are used in the baking of Christmas cookies, for example. They are symbols of the gifts of spices that the Wise Men brought to the Infant Jesus.

During the holiday of Hanukkah, people eat potato pancakes fried in oil. The pancakes are fried in oil to celebrate the miracle of one day's supply of oil burning for eight days.

Blackeyed peas, thought to bring good luck in Africa, are still served for that reason in the area of the Caribbean and in the southern United States on New Year's Eve. And what would Thanksgiving be without turkey and cranberry sauce?

The sharing of food and eating with others make people feel closer to each other. Many people do not like to eat by themselves. Those who live alone often say that food tastes much better when eaten with family or friends.

People associate certain foods with certain activities. You are probably familiar with the sound and smell of popcorn in the movie theater. Hot dogs and roasted peanuts may remind you of baseball games.

Your family may have its own food traditions. One year Joe's grandmother prepared a special chocolate dessert for a family gathering. Everybody loved it. From that day on whenever Joe's family got together, his grandmother made the dish. After Joe's grandmother died his uncle Paul took over making it. That particular dish, its taste and smell, became associated with family gatherings and good times for Joe's whole family.

Likes and Dislikes

Each of us has our own personal associations with food. You probably like some foods more than others. You may even say that you love a particular food. That may be simply because you have good memories associated with it. Maggie, who is now a grown woman, remembers the wonderful mashed potatoes her mother fed her when she was ill as a little girl. That food made her feel loved. To this day, whenever Maggie feels sick or depressed, she fixes herself fluffy mashed potatoes.

But there also foods that may make you feel sick to your stomach. Thirteen-year-old Min is not very picky about food. He eats practically everything. But Min hates peas. He hates peas so much that he feels queasy just looking at them. When Min was younger, his mother made peas for dinner almost every night and always forced him to eat them. Many of us who have similar problems with certain foods often do not know why.

Gregory, 16, loved Chinese food. Every Saturday night, his family would dine at a local Chinese restaurant. Each week Gregory looked forward to Saturday night. By Friday he was so anxious to eat the delicious food that he was certain that he could smell all of the wonderful, spicy aromas.

One Saturday night Gregory and his family ate Chinese food as usual. That evening, he came down with the worst case of stomach flu that he had ever experienced.

He was sick for days afterward. While Gregory knew that it was not the food that had made him ill, he could not help but associate Chinese food with feeling miserable.

To this day, Gregory feels uncomfortable when he sees or smells Chinese food. The experience of being sick completely changed his feelings for his favorite type of food.

What you eat also depends on how you feel. Some

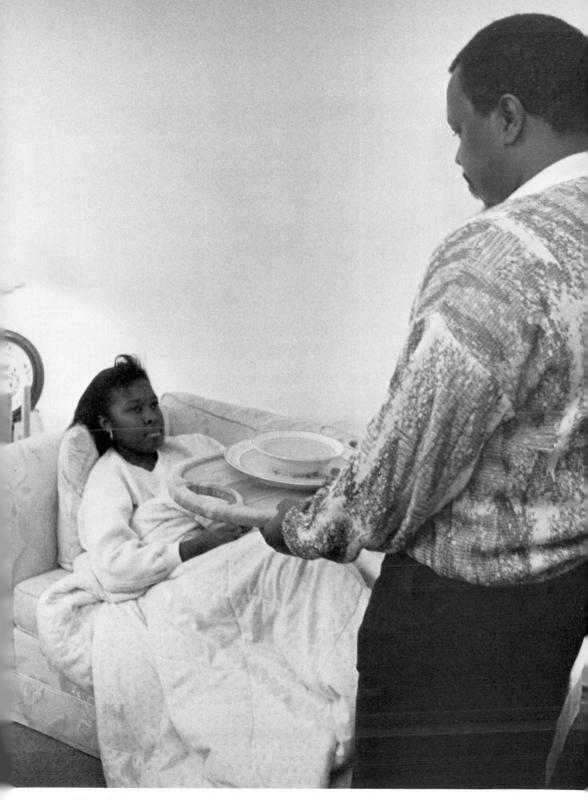

We all have certain foods that comfort us when we are upset or ill.

people stop eating when they feel nervous, scared, depressed, or lonely.

Food and Stress

Some people use food as a way to cope with stressful problems. After a particularly bad day, these people may gorge themselves on ice cream or cookies to feel better. Everyone has bad days once in a while, and there is nothing wrong with occasionally eating something that makes you feel better. However, it is unhealthy to use overeating or undereating as a way to cope with your problems. When this happens, you may be in danger of developing an eating disorder.

Fasting

Fasting means not eating or drinking for a period of time. Partial fasting means that a person avoids eating or drinking certain foods. A complete fast usually means no food or drink at all. Some people fast for political reasons; others fast for religious reasons. When someone does not eat because of political reasons, this is called a hunger strike.

There are also people who fast for health reasons. These people believe that fasting gives their body a rest from eating and digesting. However, it is important to realize that depriving the body of food for an extended period of time can be dangerous.

Chapter 2

The Weight-Control Craze

The message that many people receive from the media, especially television, movies, and advertisements, is that they need to be thin and trim to be successful and happy. As a result, many people today believe that, if they are not extremely thin, they are unattractive and undesirable.

The media often make teenagers feel pressure to be thin. With few exceptions, celebrities, models, and people in movies, on television, and in magazines have one thing in common: they are all thin. Overweight characters are infrequent on television and in films. Even if characters of above-average weight are featured, they are often not the main characters, or they are portrayed in an unflattering way.

It is important to note that the idea of what a desirable body looks like varies from society to society and even from one generation to another. There is no universally perfect body or idea of beauty. Marilyn Monroe was voluptuous, but Kate Moss is very thin. Yet each, for her own time period, is considered the beauty ideal.

A lot of people develop unhealthy eating habits during their teens. During those years, they are searching for an identity. They're in an uncertain period of their lives. Their bodies are changing, and they are very self-conscious about it.

Jasmeen, 15, was popular in school and had many friends. She was a superb violinist in her school orchestra and an editor on her school newspaper. She was an attractive girl with long black hair and a lovely complexion, but Jasmeen felt fat and ugly compared to the models in her magazines. She decided to go on a diet. She wanted to lose weight before the summer so she could show off her new figure. She wanted to lose 20 pounds in two and a half months. She figured she needed to lose about two and a half pounds each week.

She carefully outlined her diet. She bought diet pills her friends recommended. Every morning instead of eating breakfast, she would go jogging. For lunch, she would eat two carrot and celery sticks and an apple. As soon as she got home from school, she would go jogging again. She would often skip dinner.

After two months, she had lost 15 pounds. All her friends noticed the weight loss and complimented her on it, but Jasmeen was not happy. She wanted to lose more. She felt her hips and thighs were still too fat.

Her parents were concerned about her. She had become moody and irritable. She was often tired. They did not like her dieting, but they couldn't make her stop. They would often order Jasmeen to eat dinner, but even then she would eat only a couple of bites. Her parents were

A distorted body image is nearly always a part of any eating disorder.

Magazines and newspapers are filled with images of thin
people who are supposed to be the ideal of beauty for all.

*becoming increasingly alarmed at how pale Jasmeen was.
When she came home from school one day, her parents
told her they had made a doctor's appointment for her
tomorrow. Jasmeen grew angry and told her parents to
leave her alone. She refused to go to the appointment.*

*The next day, Jasmeen collapsed during her gym class.
She was rushed to the hospital. At the hospital, Jasmeen
finally admitted to herself that something was wrong, but
she was scared and didn't know what to do. She had to*

stay at the hospital for a few days to recover from mal-nourishment. During that time, she talked with her parents and her doctor about her feelings. She thought losing weight would make her feel better, but it only made her hungry and miserable all the time. Jasmeen said she had wanted to stop, but she didn't know how.

Jasmeen's doctor recommended that she see a therapist, a specialist who helps teens with eating problems. With help from her parents and her therapist, Jasmeen was able to recover.

Jasmeen was able to get on with her life. When she was able to eat normally again, she found that she had energy for her friends, her music, and her schoolwork again. She learned to be happy being herself. She came to accept that it was OK if she did not look like the models in the magazines.

Where do Jasmeen and other teenagers get the idea that they need to be thinner? It may come from their environment. While the media play a big part, people's environment also plays a big part. They may be sur-rounded by friends who talk constantly about dieting. They may see that they or overweight classmates are often made fun of.

A lot of teens also compare themselves to models in magazines and actors and actresses on television. They forget that each person is different. We each have our own style and taste, and we each have our own unique look. The world would be pretty dull if everyone looked alike.

A lot of our ideas also come from advertisements. We see lots of ads for foods promising to make us slim. Health clubs urge us to lose weight. Advertisements almost always show tall, thin, and attractive models.

People in the United States alone spend over $10 billion each year on weight-loss products. These items include diet pills, weight-loss foods and drinks, gym memberships, workout clothing, and expensive exercise machines.

People use these products with the hope of becoming thinner. However, most of them do not want to lose weight to become healthier or stronger. They want to be thinner to be more attractive.

To lose weight sensibly, you need to follow an exercise program and eat a healthy, well-balanced diet. However, if your ultimate goal is weight loss rather than better health, you may resort to unhealthy methods to lose weight. This is how an eating disorder can start. Your goal of losing weight becomes more important than anything else—including your health.

Changing Ideas of Fat and Thin

Where do we get our ideas as to how fat or thin we should be? For the past 25 years it has been fashionable to be thin. Models who wear the latest fashions in magazines have been very thin. "The thinner, the better" is how most people have tended to think about weight and beauty.

But our ideas about fatness and thinness have changed over the years. That is especially true of women's figures. Long ago, for example, it was very fashionable for women to have big hips and big

Drastic weight-loss programs can be unhealthy—even
dangerous.

breasts. Clothes were designed to show off the hips and breasts.

The words we use to describe body size tend to change, depending on how we think about fatness and thinness. When bigger was more fashionable, we used words like full-figured, plump, and cuddly to describe certain people. Today, those people would probably be called fat.

At one time being heavy was a status symbol. It was hard for many people to get enough to eat each day. If you were fat it meant that you were well off. Thinness was associated with being poor. And because the poor were often sick, being thin was also thought to be unhealthy.

More recently, however, thinness has become desirable. We use words like *slim* and *trim* for a look that in the past would have been described as skeletal and unattractive.

We are influenced by what our culture decides is fat or thin. For some of us that is a big problem. We can't fit into a mold someone else has chosen for us.

The Importance of Healthful Eating

In our drive to become thin, many of us do not eat healthfully. Each of us has a different body type and different food needs. Some people are very active. Some people spend a lot of time sitting down. Some of us are old, some very young. We have different needs at different times in our lives.

A woman who is pregnant needs to eat more than a
woman who is not. Athletes who expend a lot of
energy have to make sure they eat enough health-
ful food. When we are recuperating from illness
our bodies may require more nourishment to be
able to recover completely.

   Not eating properly can create health problems.
This is especially true of young people. Active
young people need well-nourished bodies. Young
bodies cannot grow on diet sodas that contain only
one calorie.

Plain vegetables and diet soda do not make a healthy, well-
rounded meal for a growing teen.

Restricting calories may make you thin, but it will not always be good for you. Dieting too much is more harmful to young bodies than being a little overweight.

Your job as a responsible person is to learn as much about eating healthfully as you can. There are so many things you can eat that are delicious and are good for you. You and your body need to be fed properly.

How Do You Think about Food?

1. When you haven't eaten in a long time, how do you feel physically? Do you feel tired, weak, or even faint?
2. If you are very hungry, how do you feel emotionally? Can you describe those feelings?
3. What food or foods, if any, give you a feeling of being cared for? Do you know why?
4. What are some of your favorite foods associated with family, religious, or national holidays and celebrations?
5. What food or foods, if any, do you strongly dislike? Do you remember when you first developed this dislike?
6. Do you ever eat because you are bored or feeling lonely?
7. Do you know what activities make you want to eat, whether or not you are hungry?
8. Can you name any foods with smells that you associate with certain feelings?
9. Do you ever use food to reward yourself?

Chapter 3

What Are Eating Disorders?

This book discusses two eating disorders: anorexia nervosa and bulimia nervosa. People with anorexia nervosa intentionally starve themselves to lose weight. They may eat very little food, or they may not eat any food at all.

People suffering from bulimia nervosa eat large amounts of food, called bingeing, and then use various methods to rid their bodies of it, called purging. Methods can include self-induced vomiting, taking laxatives, exercising compulsively, or any combination of these.

Teens who develop eating disorders use food as a way to exercise control over their lives or to express their emotions. They focus all their energy and attention on one goal: to lose weight. They may associate being thin with being happy, popular, and successful. Many think that, if they become thinner, their problems will disappear.

But life cannot be perfect. So if you are counting on thinness to make your life perfect, you will never feel thin enough. And you will never feel you have lost enough weight.

Anorectics do not see themselves as they really are. They never see themselves as thin, even when to others they look like living skeletons. That is part of the problem. They have a distorted image of themselves.

Historical Views of Eating Disorders

A form of what we now call anorexia was seen in the Middle Ages, over 500 years ago. Then it was called *anorexia mirabilis*. The term means a loss of appetite caused by a miracle. In those days many women refused to eat. Their fasting was considered miraculous, and they were considered very special people.

Some religious young women fasted to repent for their sins. They were admired for their ability to live on the smallest amount of food. One of these women was made a saint. She was called Saint Catherine of Siena. She ate no more than a spoonful of herbs a day. Not eating became a symbol for being especially holy and devout.

Two hundred years later that kind of fasting was no longer considered miraculous and it came to be discouraged by the Church. It was thought to be inspired by the devil. So a great effort was made to stop such behavior.

Saint Catherine of Siena expressed her religious devotion by fasting for long periods of time.

In the late 19th century, fasting and starving were looked upon in yet a different way. Science and medicine had made advances. Doctors and scientists were able to identify and name diseases. But they were not yet able to cure them.

Loss of appetite was considered a symptom of many diseases. People were thought to lose their appetite as a result of cancer, stomach diseases, and the nausea of early pregnancy. But few people believed that loss of appetite, or the refusal to eat, could actually be a disease itself.

Doctors found it hard to believe that people would deliberately starve themselves. They felt certain that a separate disease was causing this "lack of appetite." So they kept looking for physical reasons.

Sir William Withey Gull was a well-known English doctor. Around 1870, he came to the conclusion that there was a "starving disease" that began in the patient's mind. He is believed to have been the first person to call the disease anorexia nervosa. The word *nervosa* refers to the mind.

At the same time doctors in France and the United States saw and described similar cases. They came to the same conclusions as Dr. Gull.

Possible Causes

Exactly what causes the mind to "misthink" in this way is still not completely known. There may be many reasons.

Even though anorectics refuse to eat, they will often take charge of meals for other people.

Some doctors believe that one cause may be not wanting to face adulthood. By keeping his or her body thin, preventing it from growing properly, the person suffering from anorexia (or bulimia) may be expressing a fear of growing up.

Another theory is that people with eating disorders need attention. They see everyone around them struggling with their appetite. They believe that by living on practically no food they can prove themselves to be special and unique. They can feel important and boost their self-esteem.

Many people with eating disorders share certain personality traits. These include low self-esteem, feelings of helplessness or loss of control, and a fear of being fat.

A recent finding suggests that eating disorders may run in families, especially among female members. This may occur because a mother's behavior strongly influences her daughter. Studies show that mothers who place a lot of emphasis on their daughters' weight and appearance increase the risk that their daughters will develop an eating disorder.

Many people also acquire eating disorders to gain a sense of control. They often feel they lack control over their bodies and their lives. In an effort to exercise some power, they become obsessive about when and how much they eat. Another way teens with anorexia exercise control is by cooking for family and friends. This way, they can control what they and others eat.

Adolescence is also a difficult time to establish a positive self-image. Both boys and girls go through dramatic physical changes in a short time. When you are a teen, every time you look in the mirror you may see a change. You may experience a lot of ups and downs, or mood swings.

Peter was struggling to gain a good self-image. He was 15, and he wanted to be noticed. He was very bright and a good student. He was competitive in everything he did. He also tended to be critical of both friends and family. Peter was popular in school but did not have any really close friends. In that sense he was a loner.

Peter was used to getting his way at home. His parents, both busy professionals, didn't spend much time with him. They were intimidated by his constant criticism of them. They usually gave in to his demands. He was good at playing one parent against the other, but he wasn't really happy with that. He wished his parents would stand up to him. But he thought they didn't care enough for him to do so.

Peter's parents were extremely generous in buying him things and giving him money. He only had to mention that he wanted something, and there it was.

Peter took up tennis so he could play with his father and was very competitive when they played. There was never a happy ending to their games. If Peter didn't win he was totally depressed. When he did win, he thought his father hadn't tried his best. And then Peter would sulk.

Eating disorders may turn the family dinner table into a battleground.

Peter also took up running. He wanted to become really fit and thin. He wanted to become the best runner in his school. He read up on running and dieting. He followed a very rigorous training schedule. He had a long list of foods he thought were bad for him, and he continued to cut down his portions of food. Family mealtimes usually ended in a big argument.

Peter lost weight, but he still did not like the way he looked. He ate even less. He increased his running time and mileage. But even that didn't seem enough. His dieting and his running took control of him. No matter how much weight he lost and no matter how much he ran, it was never enough.

At the end of eight months Peter's weight had dropped from 135 pounds to 95 pounds. He looked like a skeleton.

It wasn't until his sister walked in on him while he was getting dressed that he realized he had a problem. He saw the look of horror on her face. For the first time, Peter took an honest look at his body and saw that his bones were sticking out of his skin. He realized that he needed help.

It wasn't easy, but Peter managed to tell his parents about the problems he was having. His parents said they thought he may have an eating disorder, and they made an appointment for him to see a doctor.

Soon afterward, Peter entered a treatment program that his doctor recommended, and he also started seeing a therapist to help him deal with his feelings.

Dieting becomes dangerous when it rules every minute of your day.

Chapter 4

Anorexia: When Dieting Goes Too Far

Just when you are most confused by all the changes happening in your body as you become an adult, you pick up messages from TV, radio, and magazine ads telling you how you ought to look. The ads are for beautiful skin, thin bodies, silky hair, and long, manicured nails. It is not possible to look like the models in the ads all the time, if ever.

Images from ads probably help bring on eating disorders. But whatever the cause, if you have an eating disorder, you should get help as quickly as possible. That is why it is important to know the symptoms of eating disorders.

The Dieting Fad

You probably know someone on a diet. That person may even be you. The word *diet* used to refer to what

someone ate on a regular basis. If you were asked
what your diet was like, you were simply being
asked what you ate day after day. Today the word
usually refers to eating in a special way in order to
lose weight.

Dieting has become very fashionable. Many
people believe that it is something they ought to do.
Dieting is often a topic of conversation.

We have been told so often that thin is good,
healthy, and beautiful. But how thin is good? And
should everyone be thin?

Fear of being fat makes people, particularly girls
and women, limit what they eat. Dieting for weight
loss is a serious business. It should never be done
without the guidance of a health professional. This
is especially true for teenagers. Teens often go on
diets to become thin. But the teen years may not
be the best time in one's life to diet for the sake of
looking thin.

Not eating properly can be bad for your health,
especially if you are growing. The food you eat
should be carefully chosen. Each meal should be
as nourishing as possible. Watching what you eat is
important not only for weight loss. It is important
because you need to eat well for your body to grow
and develop healthily.

It is not easy to be casual about dieting. If you
are dieting you may worry about whether you will
succeed. You may worry about whether you will
look as well as you had hoped after those pounds

have disappeared. You may worry about whether you will be able to keep those unwanted pounds off. All that worry can be very stressful.

When people diet they tend to think about it all the time. There is much to do. You have to weigh the food. You have to count calories and substitute some foods for others. You have to shop, cook, and bake. All that effort takes a lot of time and energy.

For some people, dieting can seem to take over their lives. They may feel out of control. That makes them stick even more strictly to their diet. And of course, if they fail to lose those pounds, they believe it is the fault of the diet. So they try another one that promises success.

People suffering from anorexia take dieting to extremes. Every waking moment is spent figuring out how to avoid eating. They have to think up excuses to explain why they barely touch their food at the dinner table. Usually they exercise a lot to lose still more weight. Even when they are terribly thin they *see* themselves as fat. It is as if the mirror tricks them and lies to them about how they look. But it is their mind that tricks them.

Beth was a beautiful girl. At 14, she was the envy of all her friends. She lived with her parents in a beautiful house. She was on the honor roll in school. She had great athletic ability, and she was musically talented. She was popular and was the president of her class. To other kids it seemed that Beth had it all!

Over the next few months her friends began to notice that she was losing a lot of weight. Thinking that she was on a diet, they complimented her on her weight loss. But then they noticed that she was not only getting very thin, but acting differently too. She was no longer available to her friends. She always managed to have an excuse for not joining them. She avoided most social activities.

At home, Beth's parents noticed changes too. They were worried by how thin she had gotten. They never saw her eat. Beth had all sorts of reasons to explain why she was never hungry. She would say that she had just had a snack. Or she would claim that she had stopped off for a pizza with friends before coming home from school. Her parents decided that she must be all right. After all, she had so much energy. She exercised a lot, and she kept up with her school work as well as her other activities.

But Beth became even thinner and paler. She began to look quite sick. Beth's mother noticed that her supply of tampons had not been touched in months. She became alarmed. She realized that Beth was ill.

Beth's mother immediately made an appointment with the family doctor. It was not easy to persuade Beth to go see the doctor. She did not believe anything was wrong with her. In fact, she was so happy with her weight loss that she planned to go on dieting. She was even convinced that she looked beautiful.

Symptoms of Anorexia Nervosa

As mentioned earlier, there are no early warning signs for anorexia. Weight loss is the first obvious sign. Most of the time we see weight loss as good. So we may actually reinforce a symptom of the disease by complimenting a person who is beginning to be ill with it.

The word anorexia means lack of appetite, but anorectics feel hunger. They may even have severe hunger pangs. But unlike the rest of us, feeling hungry makes them feel good. It reassures them that they are not gaining weight. The worst feeling for an anorectic is feeling full.

Cutting food into very tiny pieces makes it look as though the anorectic is eating.

Many anorectics adopt peculiar habits with food. They may spend a lot of time during a meal cutting food into tiny bites. They may chew the food very slowly. They may constantly drink water. Some of these habits are designed to deceive family and friends. By playing with the food while others eat, they keep busy at the table.

The most visible symptom of anorexia is the large weight loss. But after a while other symptoms appear. The skin becomes extremely dry and pale. The hair becomes brittle. If the person is a female who has begun menstruating, her periods will stop.

Anorectics may also experience frequent light-headedness, even fainting. This is usually the result of *anemia*. Anemia happens when the blood is not getting enough nourishment to create red cells. It is the red cells in the blood that carry oxygen to all the other parts of your body.

As the disease goes on and the weight gets lower, the anorectic always feels chilly. Starvation has caused the body temperature to drop. A growth of soft, downy hair develops all over the body. The hair is called *lanugo*. It is the body's way of keeping itself a little warmer.

The brain is starving too. Thinking becomes confused and unclear. The anorectic has trouble concentrating and making decisions.

At this point, the anorectic is very ill and must get help just to survive. Often a long hospital stay is needed to recover.

Chapter 5

Bulimia: Bingeing and Purging

Eating a great deal at one time and then ridding the body of the food is called *bulimia*. Bulimia is believed to be a modern disease. It was discovered in the 1950s.

Bulimia occurs about twice as often as anorexia. But it is harder to detect. Because they do eat, bulimics do not get as thin as anorectics. Bulimia is less likely to result in death. But it can make you very ill.

The Bulimic Pattern

Bulimics live with a lot of shame. They hate themselves after they *binge*. Bingeing is the word used to describe the uncontrolled eating of bulimics. When bulimics *purge*, they tend to feel disgusted with themselves. Purging is getting rid of food, by forcing oneself to vomit, for example.

Like anorectics, bulimics are terrified of being fat. At the same time, however, they have a terrific hunger for food. It is believed that their binge eating may be the result of a hunger for other things that are missing in their lives. Usually, they are not aware of what they are missing.

Some bulimics eat huge quantities of food at one time.   Others may not eat that much, but they are always disgusted with themselves for having eaten.

Bulimics make themselves vomit. They also use *laxatives* and *diuretics* (water pills). Bulimics often exercise to extremes to get rid of the food and the pounds. Unlike anorectics, who stay away from food, bulimics need to fill themselves up with food.

Purging is something bulimics must do. It is a kind of addiction. The purging controls them. Because they feel so ashamed of their behavior, bulimics want to keep it a secret. Hiding the binge eating and the purging can demand most of their time and energy.

Getting all that food and eating it without letting family and friends see becomes a real challenge to the bulimic.

Eating huge amounts of food is also expensive. Getting the money for it may become a problem.

Bulimics may have large swings in weight, but their average weight is usually normal. Because they don't look skinny, they hide their disease easily.

Bulimics "binge" by eating a lot of food and then "purge" by causing themselves to vomit.

The Dangers of Bulimia

Bulimic behavior is as dangerous to your health as anorexic starving. Bulimics are less likely to die than are anorectics, but some bulimics have choked to death on their own vomit.

Constant vomiting can cause serious damage. Large amounts of strong acid are brought up from the stomach. In the stomach, this acid aids the digestion of food. But in the mouth, this acid destroys the enamel of the teeth and causes them to rot. The gums are also affected.

Repeated vomiting can also injure the *esophagus*. The esophagus is a muscular tube about nine inches long that carries food from the mouth to the stomach. Repeated vomiting can cause the walls of this tube to tear and bleed. If the bleeding cannot be stopped promptly, it can cause death.

Using a combination of laxatives and water pills can also be fatal. A mineral imbalance occurs from the loss of so much fluid from the body. This can affect the heart rhythm.

Emily, 14, had become self-conscious about her figure. Some of her friends told her she was getting chubby. The truth was that her body was changing. Her figure was becoming fuller. This was normal for her age.

Emily's parents had a lot of fashionable friends. Emily knew how important it was to them to remain slim. She heard her parents and their friends speak unkindly about people who were fat.

Emily became afraid of getting fat. She started to diet to lose weight. But feeling hungry all the time made her miserable. Her parents traveled a lot, and she was often home alone.

One day a friend told Emily that she had found the answer to the problem of becoming fat. She told Emily how to make herself vomit and how to use laxatives and water pills. Emily was thrilled the first time she tried vomiting. The huge amount of food she had eaten was all there in the toilet bowl—instead of adding pounds to her body. She really believed that this was the greatest possible solution to the problem of becoming fat.

Sometimes it was hard to hide what she was doing. And she did feel ashamed. She also hated lying to her parents. She made up excuses to explain why she always ran from the table right after dinner.

Emily bought the laxatives and the water pills. She also began using diet pills. Some days she did nothing but purge herself. She had become addicted to the behavior. She would need a lot of help and time to recover.

Emily believed she had found the way to have a thin body through bulimic behavior. Many of us follow unhealthy patterns of eating and dieting. When we eat too much of something, we may feel guilty. We may not eat the next day. Or we may exercise too much. Many people fast for a few days when a big party is coming up. That's so they feel they can eat a lot.

Carla, 15, was a very bright and attractive girl with many friends. Carla, however, didn't feel attractive. She thought that the wide hips and broad shoulders she inherited from her father made her unattractive. She wanted to be more like her sister Sara. Carla thought that Sara was the lucky one because she had inherited their mother's petite form.

Carla decided to lose weight and become slim and dainty like her sister. She decided to cut down to one meal a day and exercise as often as she could. By the end of a week, Carla lost 3 pounds, but she felt hungry and miserable. She waited until everyone was asleep one night. Then she went down to the kitchen and stuffed herself with all the food she had cut from her diet. Because of all the food she ate, she felt so sick that she threw up.

Carla thought she had found the perfect solution. She could eat what she wanted and not gain any weight, so she started purging after every meal. Her only thought was that she would soon look like her sister.

What Carla didn't realize was that no matter how hard she tries, she will not look like her sister. They are different people who inherited different things from their parents. No amount of diet or exercise can change that. Carla was born to have wide hips and broad shoulders, just as Sara was born to have a petite form. Each is its own kind of beauty.

Chapter 6

Keeping Your Body Healthy

How do you avoid getting an eating disorder? Unfortunately, there is no *one* thing you can do that will prevent you from getting anorexia nervosa or bulimia. No vaccination or pills can keep you from getting an eating disorder.

Avoiding eating disorders takes a lot of work and awareness; the same things you would do to prevent most illnesses. You have to work at keeping yourself as healthy as you can—not only physically, but mentally healthy too.

Taking Care of Yourself

You have been given this wonderful human being—you—to take care of. This is a job for the rest of your life.

Let's look at how you can take care of your physical health. What does your body need?

You probably learned many ways to avoid getting hurt as you grew up. These reminders may sound familiar:

•Look both ways when crossing the street; cross only when the light is green.

•Buckle up when riding in a car.

•Wear a helmet when skateboarding, bike riding, or motorcycle riding.

•Wear warm clothes in winter.

•Use an effective sunscreen to prevent a summer sunburn.

Another important thing you can do for your health is to have regular medical and dental checkups. That may help to catch small problems before they become bigger problems. It is always a good idea to ask questions when you visit the doctor and the dentist. Be sure to talk about anything that is bothering you.

Exercise

Exercise is important. It will keep you fit and relaxed. Being physically active can help you let off steam and keep you feeling good. It doesn't matter what you do. It can be playing ball, dancing, running, or doing gymnastics. But it should be something you enjoy.

Always exercise in *moderation*. That means do it sensibly. Don't overdo it. You are in charge. Find out how much exercise is comfortable for you. Know your own limits.

While daily exercise is good, overexercising can cause serious problems of exhaustion, injury, and malnutrition.

Eating Healthfully

Another way to stay healthy is to eat sensibly. What is sensible eating? Here again it is a good idea to follow the road of moderation. Moderation simply means avoiding extremes. It means staying within reasonable limits. Too much of anything is not good for you.

When she was fifteen, Maria decided she would become a vegetarian. She had read that meat contained a lot of fat and cholesterol, so she figured that cutting it out of her diet would be a healthy way to lose weight.

However, after a few months Maria noticed that she was feeling tired all the time. She was horrified to discover that she was losing her hair, too.

Maria's mom made an appointment for her with the family doctor. Her doctor did a blood test. It showed that Maria was iron deficient, which was causing her fatigue and hair loss. Her doctor told her that meat was a good source of iron. He said that when Maria cut it from her diet she didn't eat anything else that provided enough iron. She didn't know it, but she was hurting her body.

Try not to label foods as fat or thin foods. Don't label foods as either bad or good. It is the way we use foods that makes them good or bad for us. There is one exception, however. If you are allergic to a certain food, any amount of that food is bad for you. It could even be deadly. But that is not the case with most foods.

Vary what you eat. We have so many choices of foods. Become an explorer. Promise yourself that you will try any new food that is offered to you. If you don't like it, don't ask for more. But if you have not tried it, you will never know whether you like it or not. If you don't like a certain food at first, try it again some other time. Your tastes will change as you get older.

It is not easy to eat right all the time. You may have a busy life, and it may be hard to eat sensibly at times. However, your body does a lot of growing and changing during the teen years. You need to provide it with a well-balanced diet for it to grow and develop properly.

A sensible diet is a well-balanced diet. Fruits, vegetables, dairy products, and protein are important to a growing body. This does not mean you can never have ice cream or cookies. A sensible diet means that you eat everything in moderation. If you had a hamburger and fries for lunch, have a lighter dinner, such as salad and soup. Try to avoid too much sugar, salt, and caffeine.

Some people say they have problems with snacking. When we think of snack foods, most of us think of the commercial snacks that come in packages. Most of these snacks are actually prepared to tease your taste buds into eating more than you need. They are very sweet or very salty, sometimes both. They often contain a lot of fat. Our taste buds like salty, sweet, and fatty foods. That is why it is hard to stop eating them.

Snacking itself is not bad. There are times when you need something between meals. But you can save money and have snacks that are good for you. If you have an allowance that you regularly spend on snack

foods, try saving it. Create your snacks with
healthier, less expensive foods. Try nuts, fresh
fruit, cheese, dried fruit, popcorn, or just plain
crackers. Cut up celery sticks, carrot sticks, or any
other vegetable you like and snack on that. You
know what time of day you usually get hungry.
Plan ahead and carry your snack with you.

Think before you eat. That way you will make
better choices.

The *way* you eat is also important. Set aside
time for relaxed, unhurried eating. Eating slowly
will help you to digest your food more easily. It also
gives you a chance to make your meals special.
Relaxed meals can be a time to look forward to.

Daily family meals—that is, meals eaten at a
certain time with most or all family members—have
become a thing of the past. Today, family meals
generally occur only on special occasions. Some
experts believe that this may have encouraged the
rise in eating disorders. Do your part in your family to have more meals together. Try to arrange for
at least one or two others to eat with you. Let your
family know that being together for meals is important to you.

Chapter 7

Keeping Your Mind Healthy

Y ou are more than just a body with different parts that have to be looked after. What makes us humans special is that all our parts are affected by everything that goes on in our bodies and in our minds. You not only have to learn to take care of your body, but also to become aware of what is happening in your mind. To avoid eating disorders, you need to stay healthy mentally.

Who Are You?

Get to know yourself. That may sound silly at first. "Of course I know myself," you may say. "After all, I am me."

But you may be surprised at how much you can learn about yourself. It can be an adventure. Try to look at yourself as others might look at you. Try the following exercise. First describe yourself.

Begin by describing your body. What does it look
like? Try not to judge yourself. You might even
want to draw a picture of yourself.

Next, describe what you are like on the inside.
Can you talk about your feelings? Do you know
what makes you happy? Do you know what makes
you sad? Do you know what you are afraid of? Do
you know what you like or dislike?

Then make two lists. Label one, "Things I Like
about Myself." Label the other, "Things I Do Not
Like about Myself."

On the "Things I Do Not Like" list put an *x* next
to the things *you* most want to change. Is your list
fair and realistic? Did you put an *x* where you
thought *someone else* might want you to change?

You may want to share your list with a friend and
have him or her do the same exercise. You may be
surprised to see how different you seem to someone else, even to someone who knows you well.

Emphasize the Positive

Many of us are too critical of ourselves. A little
self-criticism is all right. It makes us want to change
some things about ourselves. But we should not
forget all the good things about ourselves.

Remind yourself that you have many good
qualities. Give yourself frequent pats on the back.
Think about your strengths. Think often about all
the things that you do well. Then it will be easier to
remember your good qualities when you feel down.

Having a group of close friends can help to ease the emotional pain of dealing with an eating disorder.

Being a teenager is not easy. During this time, you may have to deal with difficulties in many aspects of your life. Your body is changing, and it may seem as if you have no control over these changes. You may face pressure from friends about how to act, what to wear, or whom to date. You may also feel pressure from your family about doing well in school.

You may have a hard time coping with all this stress, but keep in mind that there is always a solution to every problem. You have family, friends, teachers, and others to whom you can turn for help. No matter what happens, you are not alone.

Accept yourself as you are. Be kind to yourself. Be aware of what you can change. Also recognize the things over which you have no control.

Having Good Friends

Another way in which we grow and learn about ourselves is by creating relationships with other people. This too can be hard. Friendships take time and effort. In dealing with friends you can learn a lot about yourself. Friendships give you a chance to share both the good times and the bad times.

You have to *be* a friend to *have* a friend. You should try to avoid being too critical of your friends. Perfect friends do not exist. There will always be some disappointment and pain in dealing with the people in your life. But there will also be much satisfaction and joy in your friendships. If you develop strong friendships, your friends will be there for you when you need them.

Chapter 8

When You Need Help

If you think you may have an eating disorder, it is vital that you seek help. There are many people and places that can assist you. Speak to your parents, an older sibling, or even a teacher. You can also turn to a priest or a rabbi, a guidance counselor, a coach, or another adult that you trust. They can offer support and help you find a clinic or hospital program that specializes in eating disorder treatment. You need professional treatment to help you recover from an eating disorder.

At the clinic or treatment program, a doctor will examine you. The following conditions warrant that you be admitted immediately for treatment: rapid or excessive weight loss; serious or life-threatening physical problems; depression or risk of suicide; or severe bingeing and purging.

If the doctor believes that you have one of these symptoms, he or she will admit you as an inpatient. Being an inpatient means that you will live at the facility while you are being treated for your eating disorder.

If you don't show any of the above signs, you will be admitted as an outpatient. This means that you come to

Counselors and therapists can offer much help to teens who suffer from anorexia or bulimia. The most important step is admitting that you have a problem.

the clinic or program for treatment but are allowed to go home afterward.

In order for you to begin to recover from an eating disorder, you need to deal with the problems that initially drove you to destructive eating habits.

Therapy—both in a group and individually—can help you recognize the problems that caused your eating disorder. Therapy will also help you learn to deal with those problems in healthy ways.

What can you do if a friend or someone in your family has an eating disorder? Speak to him or her about it. Keep the tone of your voice friendly, tell him or her you're concerned, but do not accuse. Gather information about eating disorders and share it with the person. A lot of times, people with eating disorders do not know the consequences of what they are doing. Do not nag or force the person to do anything if he or she is not ready. However, if he or she does agree to seek help, be supportive. Offer to go with the person to the clinic or the doctor's office. If you are unsure about what to do, you can speak to an adult you trust, or you can write or call one of the organizations listed on page 60.

Remember, an eating disorder is a serious illness. It can cause permanent damage to the body and can lead to death. The nutritional needs of young people differ from those of adults. Young bodies are still growing and developing. Any weight loss plan that is not supervised by a health professional can damage an adolescent's body. Learn as much as you can about it. It may save your life or the life of someone you love.

Where to Go for Help

American Anorexia/Bulimia Association, Inc. (AABA)
165 West 46th Street, 1108
New York, NY 10036
(212) 575-6200
Web site:
http://members.aol.com/
amanbu/index/html

Anorexia Nervosa and Related Eating Disorders, Inc. (ANRED)
P.O. Box 5102
Eugene, OR 97405
(541) 344-1144
Web site:
http://www.anred.com

Eating Disorders Awareness and Prevention (EDAP)
603 Stewart Street, Suite 803
Seattle, WA 98101
(206) 382-3587
Web site:
http://members.aol.com/
edapinc

National Association of Anorexia Nervosa and Associated Disorders, Inc. (ANAD)
P.O. Box 7
Highland Park, IL 60035
(847) 831-3438

National Eating Disorder Organization (NEDO)
6655 South Yale Avenue
Tulsa, OK 74136
(918) 481-4044

In Canada

Anorexia Nervosa and Bulimia Association (ANAB)
767 Bayridge Drive
P.O. Box 20058
Kingston, ON K7P 1CO

Glossary

adolescence The time from puberty to adulthood.

anorexia nervosa An eating disorder in which a person eats very little food or none at all.

bulimia nervosa An eating disorder in which a person eats huge amounts of food (called bingeing) and then gets rid of it by various ways (called purging).

calorie A unit to measure the energy-producing value of food.

classify To arrange things in a certain way according to subject and category.

culture Beliefs, accomplishments, and behaviors of a group of people, passed on from one generation to another.

diuretic Something that causes someone to urinate more frequently.

epidemic The rapid spread of a disease to many people at the same time.

laxatives Something that causes someone to have more frequent bowel movements.

menstruation The periodic bleeding from the vagina, occurring usually every 28–30 days.

nourishment Food and drink needed for life.

phobia An unexplainable fear of something.

psychologist A person who has studied how the mind works.

puberty The time when the body becomes sexually mature.

recuperate To get back one's health or strength.

rigid Very strict, unchanging, and inflexible.

risk The chance of getting hurt or harmed.

ritual An act that is repeated the same way at regular intervals.

symptom Anything that is a sign of something else.

unique Being the only one of its kind.

For Further Reading

Berry, Joy. *Good Answers to Tough Questions About Weight Problems and Eating Disorders*. Chicago: Children's Press, 1990.

Bode, Janet. *Food Fight: A Guide to Eating Disorders for Pre-Teens and Their Parents*. New York: Simon and Schuster, 1997.

Crook, Marion. *Looking Good: Teenagers and Eating Disorders*. Toronto: NC Press, 1992.

Jantz, Gregory L. *Hope, Help, and Healing for Eating Disorders*. Wheaton, Ill.: Harold Shaw Publishers, 1995.

Kolodny, Nancy J. *When Food's a Foe: How You Can Confront and Conquer Your Eating Disorder*. Boston: Little Brown, 1992.

McCoy, Kathy, and Charles Wibblesman. *The New Teenage Body Book*. New York: The Body Press/Perigee Books, 1992.

Siegal, Michele, Judith Brisman, and Margot Weinshel. *Surviving an Eating Disorder: Strategies for Family and Friends*. New York: HarperPerennial, 1997.

Index

About the Author

Rachel Kubersky has a degree in library science and was a school librarian, in both primary and junior high schools. Pursuing a lifelong interest in health education, she received a master's degree in public health from New York's Hunter College. Ms. Kubersky lives in Manhattan with her husband.

Acknowledgments and Photo Credits

Cover photo by Chuck Peterson.
All other photographs by Jill Heisler Hacks, except p. 18: Stuart Rabinowitz, and p. 27: North Wind.

Design: Blackbirch Graphics, Inc.